Drawing History

ANCIENT ROME

Elaine Raphael & Don Bolognese

Scholastic Inc.

New York Toronto London Auckland Sydney

Contents

Introduction	3
Getting Started	4
Rome: From Republic to Empire	6
The Roman Forum	8
Roman Roads and Aqueducts	10
The Roman Legions	12
The Roman Alphabet	14
The Roman Colosseum	16
Roman Chariot Races	18
Spartacus: Roman Slave, Gladiator, and Rebel	20
The Roman Baths	22
A Roman Banquet	25
Roman Pompeii	27
Constantine the Great	28
A Brief History of Rome	30
Glossary	31
Index	32

ISBN 0-590-25090-6

Text and Illustrations Copyright © 1990 by Elaine Raphael and Don Bolognese.
All rights reserved. Published by Scholastic Inc., by arrangement with the author.

12 11 10 9 8 7 6 5 4 3   5 6 7 8 9/9 0/0

Printed in the U.S.A.   14

First Scholastic printing, June 1995

Introduction

According to an ancient legend, Rome was founded by the twin brothers, Romulus and Remus, who, abandoned at birth, were saved from death and raised by a she-wolf.

Whether or not the legend is true, archaeologists believe Rome began as a small village sometime around 753 B.C. Over the next few centuries it gradually gained power over its neighbors. By the time of Julius Caesar's dictatorship in 49 B.C., Rome had become the greatest power the ancient world had ever seen.

During the next few hundred years, Rome became even greater. Wherever its victorious armies went, new towns sprang up. Roman engineers built temples, public buildings, aqueducts, and roads. In the conquered lands, "All roads lead to Rome" became a popular as well as a true saying. Travel and trade became faster and safer than ever before. In Latin (the Roman language), this period from 27 B.C. to A.D. 180 was called the Pax Romana—the Roman Peace.

Listen to the sound of hobnailed sandals as a Roman legion marches out to its tour of duty.

See the bright flashes of sunlight reflected on the wings of the golden eagles held high by the legion's standard bearers.

Now, draw the proud legionary as he prepares to defend the empire.

Getting Started

This book is a guide to the history and art of ancient Rome.

The drawings and paintings are based on Roman architecture and sculpture, and the wall paintings and mosaics of ancient Pompeii and Herculaneum (Roman cities). Roman roads and buildings are so well built that some are still used today.

Much of the art of Pompeii and Herculaneum was preserved because it was buried for almost two thousand years by volcanic ash from the eruption of Mt. Vesuvius in A.D. 79.

Many of the colors in our illustrations are the colors that the Romans used, especially the bright red, which was a favorite of the Pompeiians.

The first drawing lesson is of a Roman legionary, the Roman foot soldier. He had to be in good condition to march and fight in full body armor. In addition he carried a sword, dagger, shield, and one or two spears.

If you want to know more about Roman arms and other details of Roman life, there are many beautiful and interesting books on ancient Rome. Also, museums have many fine examples of Roman art for us to enjoy.

You only need a few simple supplies to do the drawings in this book. Ordinary paper, pencils, a sharpener, and some kneaded erasers will do the job. And if you want to paint your drawings, any type of watercolor paint and brush will get you started.

1. Guidelines help you to draw figures with natural-looking proportions. Take a little extra time to make sure yours follow those in the drawing lesson before you add basic shapes.
2. Add muscle curves to legs. Notice that the soldier is shown holding his shield. It's important for artists to know such details even if they later cover or remove them.
3. Draw details of the plate armor. This type of body armor came into use at about A.D. 40. Before that, Roman soldiers wore ring mail, which was heavier and gave less protection against spears and arrows. The metal-studded

leather straps protected the lower body. Finally, erase the arm holding shield and add decorations to shield; add the spear point to shaft.

Painting

To paint one of your drawings, first transfer it to heavier paper. Here is a simple way to transfer your drawing: First rub the underside of your drawing with a soft (3B-4B) pencil. Then tape the drawing to the heavier paper. Trace your drawing with a sharp pencil. Now and then, lift a corner to see if the transfer is working. You can also use carbon paper.

When using watercolors, paint lighter colors first and darker ones last. To keep the colors clear and bright always use clean water to mix colors. Outline painted areas with a very dark pencil. You can also color your drawings with colored pencils, markers, and crayons.

Rome: From Republic to Empire

The Roman Republic forbade Roman generals from entering Rome with their legions. Roman officials hoped this would prevent an ambitious general from becoming a dictator. In 49 B.C., a powerful politician and general, Julius Caesar, ignored this law and took control of Rome.

On March 15, 44 B.C., a group of senators, who wished to bring back the Republic, assassinated Julius Caesar. A civil war followed, which ended when Octavian, Caesar's adopted son, defeated his opposition. He became the first emperor of Rome and was called Augustus. He ruled for forty-five years, a time of great prosperity and growth called the "Augustan Age." Just before his death Augustus said, "I found Rome built of sun-dried bricks; I leave it clothed in marble."

Here, Julius Caesar and his army are about to cross the Rubicon River into Roman Italy, in defiance of the Roman Senate.

1. **This is a profile of Augustus, first emperor of Rome. When drawing guidelines, notice how certain features line up with each other; top of the ear with the eye—and bottom of the earlobe with tip of the nose.**

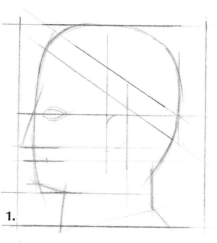
1.

2. **Add headband knot and medallions. Notice the curved lips and double chin. Roman portraits often included lifelike details.**

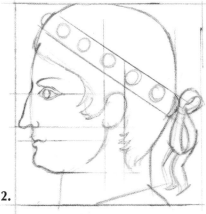
2.

3. **Put in wavy hair. Erase guidelines. Portraits like this were often used on coins.**

3.

The Roman Forum

Every Roman city had its forum. It was the center of Roman public life. It was usually a great open space ringed with temples, public buildings, and shops. In the center people listened to speeches, held religious festivals, did business, shopped, and often just passed the time of day. It was a place for celebrating victories and a place to honor famous Romans with statues and monuments.

This is a typical scene on a sunny afternoon in Rome. A poet recites verses that glorify the emperor, while Romans and visitors from faraway provinces enjoy the sights.

1. Only a Roman citizen was allowed to wear a toga. Even if you are not actually drawing the knees, elbows, and hips, you must know where they are to make the toga hang correctly.

2. The graceful folds of a toga are enjoyable to draw. Notice how the poet's left hand is holding one edge of the toga. Follow the painted figure for details in wreath and sandals.

Roman Roads and Aqueducts

In ancient Gaul (now known as France, Belgium, and the Rhineland) lived a collection of rival tribes who joined forces only to fight the Romans. But once the Romans had conquered Gaul, they united the region by improving its living conditions. The Romans built roads, aqueducts, and towns. The people of Gaul began to have a better life. They enjoyed art and drama, prosperity, and safe travel. They became part of Roman civilization.

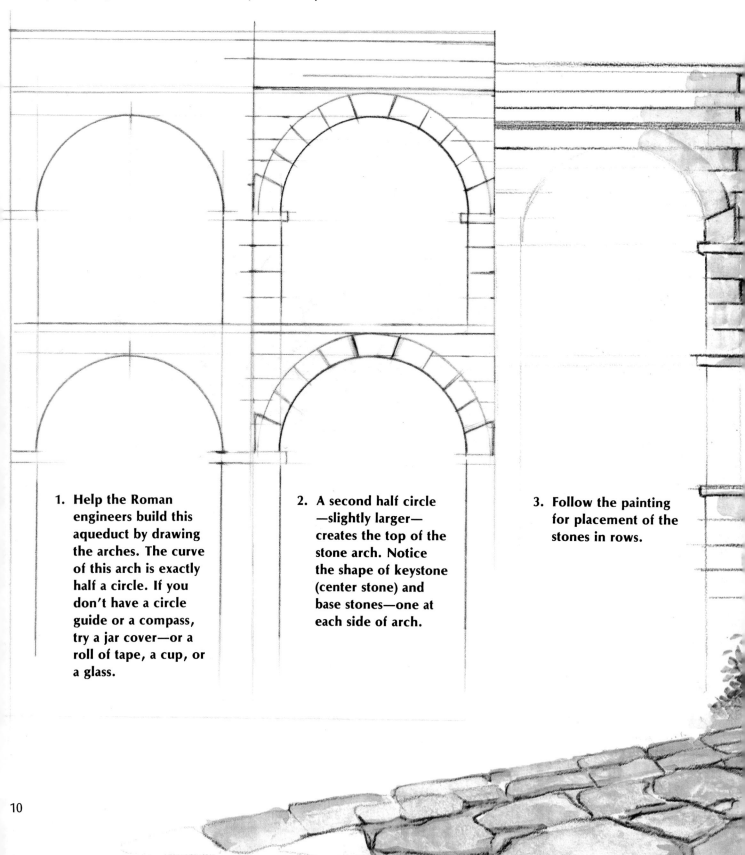

1. **Help the Roman engineers build this aqueduct by drawing the arches. The curve of this arch is exactly half a circle. If you don't have a circle guide or a compass, try a jar cover—or a roll of tape, a cup, or a glass.**

2. **A second half circle —slightly larger— creates the top of the stone arch. Notice the shape of keystone (center stone) and base stones—one at each side of arch.**

3. **Follow the painting for placement of the stones in rows.**

On a road in Gaul a Roman legion marches past a wagon carrying food to a nearby city. In the background a huge crane lifts a massive block of stone into place on a new aqueduct.

The Roman Legions

The Imperial Roman Army numbered three hundred thousand men. It was the largest, best-equipped, and most powerful fighting force in the ancient world. In addition to his armor and weapons, a legionary could depend on support from siege towers, catapults, battering rams, and an engineering corps that could build anything from a fort to a bridge.

A legionary was expected to be loyal to his officers and to the emperor. When he retired he was rewarded with a pension and a gift of land. Many towns in Roman-occupied Europe began as settlements of retired legionaries.

Here, a Roman legion attacks an enemy fort. The centurion has ordered his men into the "tortoiseshell" formation to protect them from arrows, spears, and stones as they advance toward the wall.

The legionary's basic weapon was the short stabbing sword. He carried it in a scabbard held by a leather strap (see pages 4–5). Notice the finger-hold indentations on sword handle.

The Roman Alphabet

One of Rome's most famous monuments is Trajan's Column. It is a wonderful illustrated history of the emperor's military triumphs carved in stone. At the base of the column is a large stone plaque carved with Roman letters. These Roman capital letters and others like them became models for our alphabet and typefaces. CAPITAL LETTERS like these date back to the letters at the base of Trajan's Column.

A skilled carver chisels a letter into the stone. A young apprentice watches his master's technique. Behind them a sculptor puts finishing touches on a marble statue of a Roman emperor.

The letters S P Q R on Roman monuments stand for the Latin words *Senatus Populusque Romanus*, meaning ''The Senate and People of Rome.''

1. A flat brush was used to create the letters (note the brushstrokes).

2. The letters were then outlined.

light source

3. Finally, the letters were chiseled into the stone. You can draw and paint Roman letters to look as if they were cut in stone by using shading. Notice where the light comes from—and where the shadows fall. Real gold was often applied to the carved letters to make them stand out, but you can paint your letters to resemble gold.

The Roman Colosseum

1. This view shows the Colosseum in perspective, curving away to the left. Begin with the rectangle. The guidelines help to place the ends of the curves. And notice how the curves straighten as they get closer to street level. Mark off spaces for the arches (note that they become narrower toward the left).

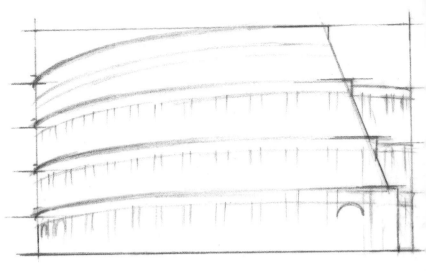

The Romans were the first to build large arches and domes. What was their secret? They discovered a new construction material so useful that it is still used today: concrete. Concrete, poured into wooden forms or molds, created the arches of the Colosseum and the dome of the Pantheon. The beauty of these and other Roman buildings has inspired architects for two thousand years. The dome on the Capitol building in Washington, D.C., is one famous example.

The great Colosseum, which could hold fifty thousand people, was used to present gladiator contests and other spectacles. Here, wild animals have been let loose in the arena before a bloodthirsty, screaming crowd. The animals will either kill each other or be killed by teams of hunters. Historians report that on the official opening day of the Colosseum five thousand animals died.

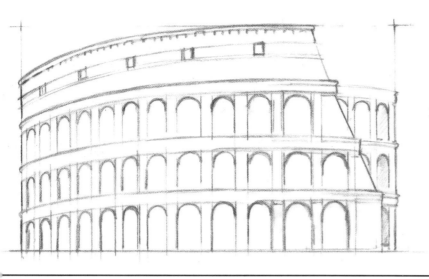

2. Use a ruler to draw vertical lines. Add circular top to arches. Each arch is separated by a column. Originally, statues stood in the arches. You may want to enlarge your drawing on a copy machine before you put in the details.

Roman Chariot Races

1. The horizontal lines help you to draw charioteer, cart, and horses in proportion to one another. Use a compass or something circular to help you draw the wheel, and a ruler for the spokes.

2. This is another drawing that you may want to enlarge before adding final details. Notice how the other horses in the team are suggested by only a few lines.

Over a million people lived in imperial Rome. Since most jobs were done by slaves, two hundred thousand Roman citizens were always out of work. For many other Romans, work ended at noon. Then there were the official holidays, sometimes as many as two hundred a year. Romans had a lot of free time. And many of them spent it at the Circus Maximus, where, every afternoon before a crowd of two hundred fifty thousand, charioteers raced for fame and fortune. Usually four teams competed, each one wearing a different color (red, blue, green, and white).

Here, a charioteer on the red team whips his four horses. He has wrapped the reins around his body so as not to lose control of them. But ahead is the turn. It is the most dangerous part of the race. A mistake could cost him his life.

Spartacus: Roman Slave, Gladiator, and Rebel

Romans loved bloody spectacles, and their favorite was gladiator contests—to the death.

Spartacus, like most gladiators, was a slave. In 73 B.C. he and a band of fellow gladiators broke out of their quarters and escaped into the countryside south of Rome. Within a short time they had an army of 90,000 slaves, a force equal to eighteen Roman legions.

The Romans feared the slave rebellion because it was a threat to their whole way of life. They sent legion after legion to capture the slaves but Spartacus defeated every one. Finally, in 71 B.C., three Roman armies trapped Spartacus. They killed him and crucified his followers as a warning to other slaves.

Here, Spartacus, wearing Thracian armor, turns on his Roman guards. Each of the other gladiators wears a special type of armor. The man with the net and trident is called a retiarius.

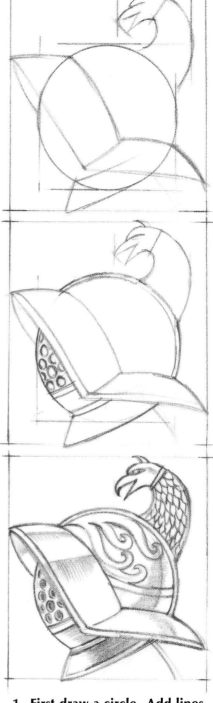

1. First draw a circle. Add lines for brim, collar, and griffin (a mythical creature) ornament.
2. Add a line to give more weight to the crown. Put in small openings in face mask.
3. Draw the designs on the crown and the scales on the griffin's neck. Shade crown and brim lightly to make helmet appear round. Put dark shadows on collar and in face-mask openings.

The Roman Baths

Roman public bathhouses were more than just places for people to get clean. They were an important part of Roman social life. Both men and women went to them either at separate places or at different times.

A Roman first undressed, then was rubbed with oil. A warm bath was next, followed by a stay in the steam room. The bather cooled down in a warm room and finished off with a plunge into a pool of cool water.

But baths also had gardens, courtyards, and gymnasiums. There were also shops, restaurants, galleries of art, and even libraries and reading rooms.

1. **Begin with the vertical line to position the feet. Then add horizontal lines for knees, waist, shoulders, etc. Lightly sketch in the figure.**

2. **If the proportions seem right, strengthen figure outlines. Add folds to tunic. The tunic was the basic garment for everyone (usually knee length for men and ankle length for women). Tone on the towels gives them more bulk.**

All this leisure and recreation were provided free to all citizens—rich and poor, noble and working class.

Here, a young slave brings fresh towels to the bathers. In the foreground, two boys play at knucklebones while an older boy lifts weights.

A Roman Banquet

Wealthy Romans enjoyed inviting friends to their homes for banquets.

Everyone reclined on couches arranged in a U shape around a low table. Musicians entertained the guests while servants brought in dish after dish. Each course was set on the table for the diners to take and eat with their fingers.

A Roman banquet was similar to a formal dinner given today. It began with very tasty appetizers, such as salty fish and eggs. The second or main course included fish, meat, and poultry. Finally came the sweets—or as we say, dessert.

At tonight's banquet the main course includes roast boar, dormice stuffed with pork and pigeons, roast parrot, and flamingo boiled with dates.

1. **A favorite hairstyle of wealthy Roman women. Curling tongs and pins were used to create it. Notice how high the front is; it's equal to the space between chin and forehead.**

2. **Add curls. The rows of braided hair at the back were often extra hairpieces made from the hair of slaves. Wreaths and gold and jeweled headbands were also favored by the Romans.**

Roman Pompeii

At 1:00 P.M. on August 24, A.D. 79, Mount Vesuvius, a long-dormant volcano overlooking the Roman city of Pompeii, suddenly erupted. Within hours this lively and beautiful city became an ash-covered tomb. Two thousand people died; the survivors fled—never to return.

For almost two thousand years Pompeii's villas, sculpture, paintings, temples, and marketplaces remained buried and untouched. When archaeologists uncovered the city they even found bread, baked that day, in the ovens. The ruins show us that everyday life in Pompeii was like ours today. Houses even had watchdogs; they had warning signs done in mosaic tile that say CAVE CANEM—Latin for "Beware of Dog."

In their atrium, a Pompeiian mother and daughter stare in shock at the towering column of fiery ash pouring from Vesuvius.

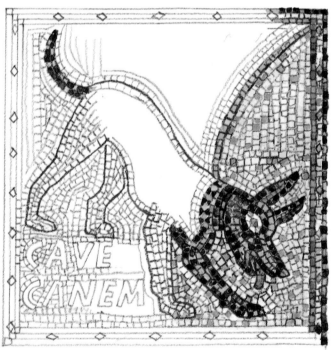

1. A mosaic is made of little squares of colored ceramic tile. It was a very popular form of art in ancient times, especially in Rome. Designing a mosaic is simple. First sketch in the basic shape of the dog. Then break up the figure into small squares. Do the same with the background. Notice that the rows of mosaic pieces follow the form of the dog.

2. After you've drawn all the squares (it takes time) add tones of gray or color to create the full picture. But first try this idea. On a copy machine make copies of your basic mosaic drawing. Now you can experiment with different colors and still have your basic drawing. Another idea: enlarge your picture and fill it with squares of colored paper instead of paint.

Constantine the Great

One night during the year A.D. 312, on the outskirts of Rome, two opposing Roman generals prepared their armies for battle. The winner would become emperor of Rome.

That night one of the generals, named Constantine, saw a vision in the form of a cross. Believing this was a sign that the Christian god would give him victory, Constantine ordered his soldiers to paint crosses on their shields.

Constantine won the battle. He soon legalized Christianity, ending a long history of Roman persecution of the Christians. Constantine also founded a "new Rome" in Byzantium, later called Constantinople. Today it is known as Istanbul, a city in Turkey.

Here, Constantine and his army prepare to go into battle under their new protector.

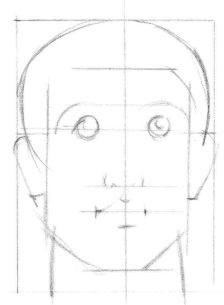

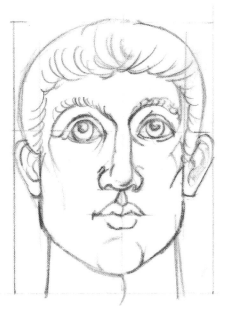

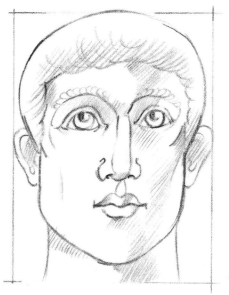

This illustration is copied from an ancient sculpture of Constantine the Great in the Metropolitan Museum of Art in New York City.

1. **While you put in the basic guidelines notice that Constantine had an unusually long rectangular head and large, round eyes.**

2. **Draw the features—lightly at first. Note the way eyelids are drawn. Emphasize the strong jaw and curved full lips.**

3. **Try this: Put a piece of tracing paper over your drawing. Add shading (as in figure 3). Do you like it? Now draw the shading on your drawing. That's another way to experiment without ruining your original.**

A Brief History of Rome

Soon after Rome was founded around 750 B.C. it came under the influence of the Etruscans. They were great sea traders, fine metalworkers, and horse breeders. Some of Rome's early rulers were Etruscans. They taught Romans about city planning, aqueducts, and road building. Rome even adopted many Etruscan beliefs concerning religion and art.

By 500 B.C. Romans were tired of kings. They formed a republic with a senate and other elected officials.

As Rome grew more powerful it also acquired a rival—Carthage. This ancient city-state on Africa's north coast fought Rome for over sixty years, from 264 B.C. to 202 B.C. Its most famous general, Hannibal, attacked Rome by crossing the Alps with an army that included elephants. Eventually Carthage was defeated, its city destroyed, and 50,000 of its survivors were taken to Rome as slaves.

By 146 B.C., six hundred years from its founding, Rome ruled over the ancient world that surrounded the Mediterranean Sea. In Rome political power began to pass from the senators to powerful individual politicians. Finally, in 44 B.C., Julius Caesar declared himself "dictator for life." A group of senators killed him, but it was too late to save the Republic. In 27 B.C., Caesar's adopted son became the Emperor Augustus.

For the next two hundred years the Roman Empire ruled without serious opposition. However, nations on Rome's border were growing stronger and more jealous of Rome's wealth. Over the next three hundred years Rome endured many invasions from people they called barbarians. One of the most famous was Attila the Hun. In A.D. 476, a Hun called Odoacer captured Rome and sent the last true Roman emperor, a fourteen-year-old boy named Romulus Augustulus, into exile.

The last remaining part of the Roman Empire ended when Constantinople, the eastern capital of the Roman Empire, was captured by the Turks in 1453.

Glossary

Aqueduct A structure for conveying flowing water.

Archaeologist A person who specializes in the scientific study of ancient civilizations.

Atrium The central hall of a Roman house.

Attila the Hun Leader of a tribe that originated in Asia and invaded the Roman Empire.

Augustus First emperor of Rome.

Boar Male pig.

Byzantium The ancient name for Istanbul, Turkey.

Carthage Ancient city on the north African coast.

Centurion A captain in the Roman army.

Circus Maximus Racetrack in ancient Rome.

Colosseum Amphitheater in Rome.

Constantine Emperor of Rome, founder of Constantinople.

Dome A roof or a ceiling having a rounded form.

Etruscan A native of Etruria (ancient area in northern Italy).

Forum The market or public place of a city.

Hannibal Famous general of Carthage.

Herculaneum Ancient city covered by volcanic ash from Mt. Vesuvius.

Julius Caesar Roman politician and general.

Knucklebones An ancient game.

Legionary Roman infantry soldier.

Mosaic A design made up of small pieces of colored glass or tile.

Pompeii Ancient city buried in volcanic ash from Mt. Vesuvius.

Pantheon Temple in Rome dedicated to all the gods.

Remus and Romulus Twin brothers who were the legendary founders of Rome.

Rubicon River River in northern Italy.

Spartacus Gladiator who led rebellion against Rome.

Thracian A native of Thrace (an area in Eastern Europe).

Trajan Emperor of Rome.

Trident A three-pronged spear.

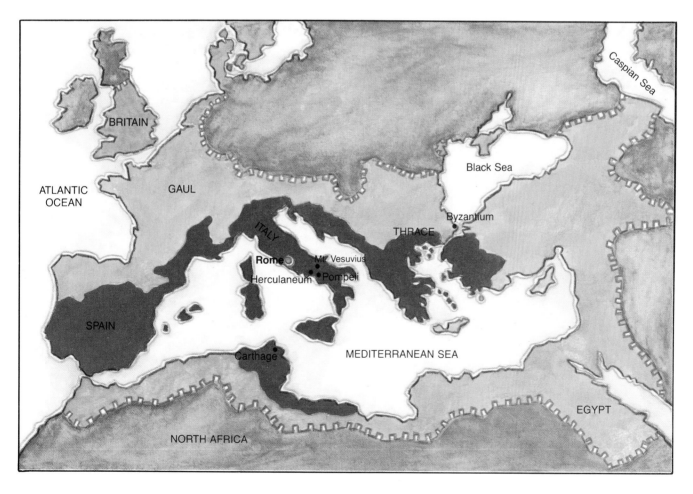

 Roman territory, B.C. 100

Roman territory at the time of Emperor Trajan, 114 A.D.

Index

Alphabet, 14–15
Animals, in Colosseum, 16–17
Aqueducts, 3, 10–11, 30
Archaeologists, 27
Arches, 10, 16, 17
Armor, 4–5, 20–21
Attila the Hun, 30
Augustus, Emperor, 7, 30

Banquets, 24–25
Baths, 22–23
Byzantium, 28

Caesar, Julius, 3, 6–7, 30
Capitol building, U.S., 16
Carthage, 30
Chariot races, 18–19
Christianity, 28
Circus Maximus, 19
Civil war, 7
Coins, 7
Colors, 4
Colosseum, 16–17
Concrete, 16
Constantine the Great, Emperor, 28–29
Constantinople, 28, 30

Domes, 16

Etruscans, 30

Forum, 8–9

Gaul, 10–11
Gladiator contests, 16, 20–21

Hairstyles, 25
Hannibal, 30
Helmets, 21
Herculaneum, 4
Horses, chariots drawn by, 18–19

Keystones, 10
Knucklebones, 23

Legionaries, 3, 4–5, 6, 11, 12–13, 21

Mosaics, 26–27

Odoacer, 30

Painting, 5
Pantheon, 16
Pax Romana, 3
Plate armor, 4–5
Pompeii, 4, 26–27

Remus, 3

Retiarius, 21
Roads, 3, 4, 10–11, 30
Rome:
    brief history of, 30
    first emperor of, 7
    founding of, 3
    territory ruled by, 31
Romulus, 3
Romulus Augustulus, Emperor, 30
Rubicon River, 7

Senate, 7
Shields, 4–5
Slaves, 19, 22, 23, 30
    rebellion of, 20–21
Spartacus, 20–21
Spears, 4–5
S P Q R, 14–15
Stone, chiseling letters into, 14–15
Supplies, 4
Swords, 4–5, 13

Thracian armor, 20, 21
Togas, 8
Tortoiseshell formation, 12, 13
Towns, 3, 10, 13
Trajan's Column, 14
Tunics, 22

Vesuvius, Mount, 4, 26–27